50 Tokyo Street Bites

By: Kelly Johnson

Table of Contents

- Takoyaki (Octopus Balls)
- Okonomiyaki (Japanese Savory Pancake)
- Taiyaki (Fish-shaped Pastry)
- Korokke (Japanese Croquettes)
- Gyoza (Japanese Dumplings)
- Senbei (Rice Crackers)
- Dango (Grilled Skewered Rice Dumplings)
- Kakigori (Shaved Ice with Syrup)
- Onigiri (Rice Balls)
- Yaki Imo (Roasted Sweet Potato)
- Negiyaki (Scallion Pancake)
- Mochi (Rice Cake)
- Agedashi Tofu (Fried Tofu in Broth)
- Takoyaki Bun
- Taiyaki Ice Cream
- Kibi Dango (Chewy Rice Candy)
- Nikuman (Pork Buns)

- Choco Banana Crepes
- Kushi Katsu (Deep-fried Skewers)
- Ikayaki (Grilled Squid)
- Korokke Sandwich
- Tempura Shrimp on Skewers
- Oden (Hot Pot with Various Ingredients)
- Shioyaki (Salt-grilled Fish)
- Gyaru-fried Sweet Potato Fries
- Japanese Pancake (Dorayaki)
- Yaki Tori (Grilled Chicken Skewers)
- Sushi Rolls (Street Style)
- Ramen Burger
- Edamame Beans with Sea Salt
- Zaru Soba (Cold Soba Noodles)
- Sweet Potato Pie
- Tofu Donburi
- Hokkaido Cream Puffs
- Mentaiko (Spicy Cod Roe) on Rice
- Japanese French Fries

- Yuba (Tofu Skin) Snack
- Shoyu Ice Cream
- Sweet Red Bean Paste-filled Buns
- Yaki Udon
- Matcha-flavored Mochi
- Japanese Street Pizza (Okonomiyaki-style)
- Baked Custard Pudding
- Dorayaki (Red Bean Pancake)
- Jaga Bata (Potatoes with Butter and Soy Sauce)
- Anko-filled Taiyaki
- Asparagus Wrapped in Bacon
- Tempura Fish Balls
- Japanese Cheese Tarts
- Rice Paper Spring Rolls

Takoyaki (Octopus Balls)

Ingredients:

- 1/2 lb octopus, cooked and chopped into small pieces
- 1 1/2 cups takoyaki flour (or plain flour with 1 tsp baking powder)
- 1 egg
- 1 1/2 cups dashi stock (or water)
- 1 tbsp soy sauce
- 1 tbsp mirin
- 1 tbsp pickled ginger, chopped
- 2 tbsp green onions, chopped
- Takoyaki sauce (for drizzling)
- Bonito flakes (for topping)
- Aonori (seaweed powder) for garnish
- Oil for greasing the takoyaki pan

Instructions:

1. In a bowl, mix takoyaki flour, egg, dashi stock, soy sauce, and mirin to form a batter.
2. Heat a takoyaki pan over medium heat and grease the holes with oil.
3. Pour the batter into each hole, filling them completely.
4. Add a piece of octopus, a bit of pickled ginger, and green onions to each hole.

5. Cook for a few minutes, then use a skewer to flip the balls 90 degrees. Keep rotating the takoyaki until they are golden brown and crispy on the outside.

6. Drizzle with takoyaki sauce, sprinkle bonito flakes, and garnish with aonori. Serve hot.

Okonomiyaki (Japanese Savory Pancake)

Ingredients:

- 1 cup all-purpose flour
- 1/2 cup dashi stock (or water)
- 1 egg
- 2 cups shredded cabbage
- 1/4 cup green onions, chopped
- 1/4 cup cooked pork belly or bacon, chopped (optional)
- 2 tbsp soy sauce
- Okonomiyaki sauce (for drizzling)
- Kewpie mayonnaise (for drizzling)
- Aonori (seaweed powder) for garnish
- Bonito flakes for garnish

Instructions:

1. In a large bowl, whisk the flour, dashi stock, egg, and soy sauce to make a batter.
2. Fold in the shredded cabbage, green onions, and cooked pork (if using).
3. Heat a griddle or non-stick pan over medium heat and grease it lightly with oil.
4. Pour the batter into the pan, forming a round pancake. Cook for 4-5 minutes on one side until golden brown, then flip and cook for another 4-5 minutes on the other side.

5. Drizzle with okonomiyaki sauce and kewpie mayonnaise, then sprinkle with bonito flakes and aonori. Serve hot.

Taiyaki (Fish-shaped Pastry)

Ingredients:

- 1 cup all-purpose flour
- 2 tbsp sugar
- 1 tsp baking powder
- 1/2 tsp salt
- 1/2 cup milk
- 1 egg
- 2 tbsp melted butter
- 1/2 cup red bean paste (anko) or custard (for filling)
- Oil for greasing the taiyaki mold

Instructions:

1. In a bowl, mix the flour, sugar, baking powder, and salt.
2. Add the milk, egg, and melted butter, stirring until smooth.
3. Grease a taiyaki mold with oil and heat it over medium heat.
4. Spoon a small amount of batter into each side of the mold. Add a dollop of red bean paste or custard, then cover with more batter.
5. Close the mold and cook for 3-4 minutes on each side until golden brown.
6. Remove from the mold, serve warm, and enjoy!

Korokke (Japanese Croquettes)

Ingredients:

- 2 medium potatoes, peeled and boiled
- 1/2 lb ground beef or pork (optional)
- 1/4 cup onion, finely chopped
- 1/4 cup flour
- 1 egg, beaten
- 1/2 cup breadcrumbs
- Salt and pepper to taste
- Oil for frying

Instructions:

1. Mash the boiled potatoes in a bowl and set aside.
2. In a pan, cook the ground meat and onion over medium heat until browned. Season with salt and pepper.
3. Mix the cooked meat and onion into the mashed potatoes.
4. Shape the mixture into small patties, then coat them with flour, dip in the beaten egg, and coat with breadcrumbs.
5. Heat oil in a deep pan or fryer over medium heat. Fry the croquettes until golden brown and crispy, about 3-4 minutes.
6. Remove and drain on paper towels. Serve with tonkatsu sauce or your favorite dipping sauce.

Gyoza (Japanese Dumplings)

Ingredients:

- 1/2 lb ground pork
- 1/4 cup cabbage, finely chopped
- 1/4 cup green onions, chopped
- 1 tbsp garlic, minced
- 1 tbsp ginger, minced
- 2 tbsp soy sauce
- 1 tbsp sesame oil
- Gyoza wrappers (available in Asian markets)
- Oil for frying

Instructions:

1. In a bowl, combine the ground pork, cabbage, green onions, garlic, ginger, soy sauce, and sesame oil. Mix well.
2. Place a small spoonful of the mixture in the center of each gyoza wrapper. Wet the edges of the wrapper with water and fold in half to seal, creating a pleated edge.
3. Heat oil in a frying pan over medium heat. Place the gyoza in the pan and cook for 2-3 minutes until the bottoms are golden brown.
4. Add a small amount of water to the pan and cover, letting the gyoza steam for another 4-5 minutes.
5. Serve with soy sauce or vinegar for dipping.

Senbei (Rice Crackers)

Ingredients:

- 1 cup glutinous rice flour
- 1 tbsp sugar
- 1/4 tsp salt
- 1 tbsp soy sauce
- 1/4 cup water
- 1 tbsp sesame seeds (optional)

Instructions:

1. In a bowl, mix the rice flour, sugar, salt, soy sauce, and water to form a dough.
2. Roll the dough into small balls, then flatten them into thin discs.
3. Heat a non-stick pan over medium heat and cook the rice discs for 2-3 minutes on each side until lightly golden.
4. If desired, sprinkle with sesame seeds for extra flavor.
5. Serve as a crunchy snack.

Dango (Grilled Skewered Rice Dumplings)

Ingredients:

- 1 cup glutinous rice flour
- 1/2 cup water
- 1/4 cup sugar
- 1 tbsp soy sauce (for dipping)
- Bamboo skewers

Instructions:

1. Mix the rice flour and water to form a dough.
2. Roll the dough into small balls and shape them into dumplings.
3. Boil a pot of water and drop the dumplings in, cooking for 3-4 minutes until they float.
4. Skewer the cooked dumplings on bamboo sticks.
5. Grill the skewers on a pan or grill for 2-3 minutes on each side until slightly crispy.
6. Brush with soy sauce or drizzle with sweet soy sauce (for a sweeter version).

Kakigori (Shaved Ice with Syrup)

Ingredients:

- Ice (preferably crushed)
- Syrup (flavors like strawberry, matcha, or condensed milk)
- Toppings like red bean paste, mochi, or fruit (optional)

Instructions:

1. Shave the ice into fine, fluffy snow using a shaved ice machine or manually.
2. Serve the shaved ice in a bowl.
3. Drizzle your choice of syrup over the top.
4. Add toppings like mochi, red bean paste, or fruit if desired.
5. Serve immediately for a refreshing summer treat.

Onigiri (Rice Balls)

Ingredients:

- 2 cups cooked rice (preferably short-grain Japanese rice)
- 1 tbsp soy sauce
- 1 tsp salt
- Filling options: pickled plum (umeboshi), cooked salmon, tuna mayo, or any filling of your choice
- Nori (seaweed) sheets for wrapping (optional)

Instructions:

1. Season the cooked rice with soy sauce and salt.
2. Wet your hands with water and take a small portion of rice.
3. Place a filling in the center and shape the rice into a triangle or round ball.
4. Optionally, wrap the rice ball with a piece of nori.
5. Serve immediately or wrap in plastic for later consumption.

Yaki Imo (Roasted Sweet Potato)

Ingredients:

- 2-3 medium sweet potatoes (Japanese satsumaimo if available)

Instructions:

1. Preheat the oven to 375°F (190°C).

2. Wash the sweet potatoes and pierce them with a fork several times.

3. Place the sweet potatoes on a baking sheet and roast for 45-60 minutes, or until tender when pierced with a fork.

4. Let cool slightly before serving. Serve as a warm and healthy snack.

Negiyaki (Scallion Pancake)

Ingredients:

- 1 cup all-purpose flour
- 1/4 tsp salt
- 1/2 cup warm water
- 1 tbsp sesame oil
- 1 bunch green onions (scallions), finely chopped
- Oil for frying

Instructions:

1. In a bowl, combine the flour and salt. Gradually add the warm water and stir until the dough comes together.
2. Knead the dough for about 5-7 minutes, then cover with a damp cloth and let rest for 30 minutes.
3. Roll the dough into a thin circle on a lightly floured surface.
4. Brush the surface with sesame oil, then sprinkle the chopped green onions evenly on top.
5. Roll the dough into a log and then shape it into a coil. Roll it out again into a thin circle.
6. Heat a little oil in a pan over medium heat and fry the pancake until golden and crispy on both sides.
7. Serve hot with soy sauce or ponzu for dipping.

Mochi (Rice Cake)

Ingredients:

- 1 cup sweet rice (mochi rice)
- 1/4 cup water
- 1/4 cup sugar (optional)
- Cornstarch or potato starch for dusting

Instructions:

1. Wash the mochi rice thoroughly and soak it in water for 4-6 hours or overnight.
2. Steam the soaked rice in a bamboo steamer for about 30-45 minutes until soft and sticky.
3. Once the rice is cooked, transfer it to a large bowl and mash it with a pestle or a sturdy spoon while it is still hot.
4. If desired, add sugar to the rice while mashing it to sweeten the mochi.
5. Once mashed, dust a clean surface with cornstarch. Wet your hands with water and form the mochi into small balls or desired shapes.
6. Coat the mochi in more cornstarch to prevent sticking.
7. Serve immediately or store in an airtight container.

Agedashi Tofu (Fried Tofu in Broth)

Ingredients:

- 1 block firm tofu, drained and cut into cubes
- 1/4 cup potato starch (or cornstarch)
- Oil for frying
- 1/4 cup dashi stock
- 2 tbsp soy sauce
- 1 tbsp mirin
- 1 tbsp grated daikon (optional)
- Green onions for garnish

Instructions:

1. Coat the tofu cubes evenly with potato starch.
2. Heat oil in a deep frying pan or pot over medium heat. Fry the tofu until golden and crispy, about 3-4 minutes on each side.
3. In a separate pan, combine dashi stock, soy sauce, and mirin. Bring to a simmer.
4. To serve, place the fried tofu cubes in a bowl, then pour the hot broth over them.
5. Garnish with grated daikon and green onions. Serve immediately.

Takoyaki Bun

Ingredients:

- 1 batch of takoyaki (see previous recipe)
- 1 batch of soft bread dough (for buns)
- Takoyaki sauce for drizzling
- Kewpie mayonnaise for drizzling
- Bonito flakes for garnish

Instructions:

1. Prepare the takoyaki as per the recipe instructions, making small octopus balls.
2. Roll out the bread dough and place a small piece of takoyaki in the center of each dough portion.
3. Pinch the edges together to seal, forming a bun around the takoyaki.
4. Place the buns on a baking sheet and bake according to the bread dough recipe instructions until golden brown.
5. Drizzle with takoyaki sauce and mayonnaise, then garnish with bonito flakes before serving.

Taiyaki Ice Cream

Ingredients:

- 2 taiyaki pastries (see previous recipe for taiyaki)
- Ice cream (flavor of choice, such as vanilla, matcha, or red bean)

Instructions:

1. Prepare taiyaki according to the recipe or purchase pre-made taiyaki.
2. Once the taiyaki has cooled slightly, cut it in half horizontally.
3. Scoop ice cream into one half of the taiyaki and gently press the other half of the pastry on top to form a sandwich.
4. Serve immediately and enjoy this fun, ice cream-filled twist on the classic taiyaki.

Kibi Dango (Chewy Rice Candy)

Ingredients:

- 1/2 cup rice flour (sweet rice flour or mochiko)
- 1/4 cup sugar
- 1/4 cup water
- 1/2 tsp vanilla extract (optional)

Instructions:

1. In a saucepan, combine the rice flour, sugar, and water. Stir to dissolve the sugar.
2. Heat the mixture over low heat, stirring constantly to prevent lumps from forming.
3. Continue cooking for about 5-7 minutes until the mixture thickens and becomes glossy.
4. Remove from heat and add vanilla extract, if using.
5. Pour the mixture onto a lightly greased surface and let it cool slightly.
6. Once cool enough to handle, shape the mixture into small, bite-sized balls.
7. Let the kibi dango cool completely before serving.

Nikuman (Pork Buns)

Ingredients:

- 1 lb ground pork
- 2 tbsp soy sauce
- 1 tbsp sugar
- 1 tbsp sesame oil
- 1/2 onion, finely chopped
- 1 tbsp grated ginger
- 1 package of bao dough (or homemade steamed bun dough)

Instructions:

1. In a bowl, combine ground pork, soy sauce, sugar, sesame oil, chopped onion, and grated ginger.
2. Roll out the bao dough into small circles.
3. Place a spoonful of the pork mixture in the center of each dough circle.
4. Pinch the edges of the dough together to seal the bun.
5. Steam the buns in a bamboo steamer or a pot with a steamer insert for 10-15 minutes, until cooked through.
6. Serve the nikuman hot with soy sauce or chili oil.

Choco Banana Crepes

Ingredients:

- 1 cup all-purpose flour
- 1 egg
- 1 cup milk
- 2 tbsp sugar
- 1/2 tsp vanilla extract
- 2 bananas, sliced
- 1/2 cup chocolate sauce or Nutella
- Whipped cream (optional)

Instructions:

1. In a bowl, whisk together flour, egg, milk, sugar, and vanilla extract to form a smooth batter.
2. Heat a non-stick pan over medium heat and lightly grease it.
3. Pour a small amount of batter into the pan and swirl it around to form a thin crepe. Cook for 1-2 minutes on each side until lightly golden.
4. Once cooked, remove the crepe and fill with sliced bananas and a drizzle of chocolate sauce or Nutella.
5. Roll up the crepe and serve with whipped cream, if desired.

Kushi Katsu (Deep-fried Skewers)

Ingredients:

- 1/2 lb chicken breast, cut into bite-sized pieces
- 1/2 lb pork loin, cut into bite-sized pieces
- 1/2 lb vegetables (such as mushrooms, bell peppers, or onions), cut into pieces
- 1 cup panko breadcrumbs
- 1/2 cup flour
- 2 eggs, beaten
- Oil for frying
- Kushi katsu sauce or tonkatsu sauce for dipping

Instructions:

1. Thread the chicken, pork, and vegetables onto wooden skewers.
2. Dredge each skewer in flour, then dip into beaten egg, and finally coat in panko breadcrumbs.
3. Heat oil in a deep pan or fryer to 350°F (175°C).
4. Fry the skewers in batches until golden brown and crispy, about 3-4 minutes.
5. Drain on paper towels and serve with kushi katsu sauce or tonkatsu sauce for dipping.

Ikayaki (Grilled Squid)

Ingredients:

- 1 whole squid, cleaned and scored
- 2 tbsp soy sauce
- 1 tbsp mirin
- 1 tbsp sugar
- 1 tsp sake
- 1/2 tsp grated ginger (optional)

Instructions:

1. Prepare the squid by cleaning it and scoring the body in a crisscross pattern.
2. In a small bowl, mix the soy sauce, mirin, sugar, sake, and grated ginger (if using) to make the marinade.
3. Brush the squid with the marinade and let it marinate for 15-20 minutes.
4. Grill the squid on a hot grill or under a broiler for 2-3 minutes per side, until slightly charred and cooked through.
5. Serve immediately, optionally with a squeeze of lemon.

Korokke Sandwich

Ingredients:

- 4 korokke (Japanese croquettes)
- 2 soft sandwich rolls
- Shredded lettuce
- Kewpie mayonnaise
- Tonkatsu sauce

Instructions:

1. Prepare the korokke by following the korokke recipe or using store-bought croquettes.
2. Cut the sandwich rolls in half and toast them lightly if desired.
3. Spread Kewpie mayonnaise on the bottom half of each roll and drizzle with tonkatsu sauce.
4. Place a korokke on each sandwich roll, top with shredded lettuce, and close the sandwich.
5. Serve immediately.

Tempura Shrimp on Skewers

Ingredients:

- 12 large shrimp, peeled and deveined
- 1 cup tempura flour
- 1 egg
- 1 cup cold sparkling water
- Oil for frying
- Salt for seasoning

Instructions:

1. Thread shrimp onto skewers, ensuring they are secure.
2. In a bowl, mix tempura flour and egg, then slowly add cold sparkling water to make a batter.
3. Heat oil in a deep frying pan or wok to 350°F (175°C).
4. Dip each shrimp skewer into the tempura batter, making sure it's well-coated.
5. Fry the shrimp skewers for 2-3 minutes or until golden and crispy.
6. Remove from oil and drain on paper towels. Season with a pinch of salt and serve with dipping sauce.

Oden (Hot Pot with Various Ingredients)

Ingredients:

- 4 cups dashi stock
- 2 tbsp soy sauce
- 1 tbsp mirin
- 1 tbsp sugar
- 1 daikon radish, peeled and cut into thick slices
- 4 boiled eggs
- 4 pieces of konjac (yam cake), sliced
- 6 fish cakes (chikuwa or hanpen)
- 1 block of tofu, cut into large cubes
- 1 pack of Japanese-style fish balls (oden balls)

Instructions:

1. In a large pot, bring the dashi stock to a boil. Add soy sauce, mirin, and sugar to the stock.
2. Add the daikon slices and simmer for 15-20 minutes until they begin to soften.
3. Add the boiled eggs, konjac, fish cakes, tofu, and fish balls into the pot.
4. Let everything simmer gently for 30-40 minutes, allowing the flavors to meld together.
5. Serve hot, with a side of mustard or chili pepper for dipping.

Shioyaki (Salt-grilled Fish)

Ingredients:

- 2 whole fish (mackerel, saba, or any preferred fish)
- 1 tbsp sea salt
- 1 lemon (optional)

Instructions:

1. Clean and gut the fish if necessary, then pat them dry with paper towels.
2. Sprinkle the fish generously with sea salt on both sides, pressing it gently into the flesh.
3. Preheat your grill or grill pan over medium heat.
4. Grill the fish for about 5-6 minutes on each side or until the skin is crispy and the flesh is fully cooked.
5. Serve the fish with lemon wedges on the side for squeezing.

Gyaru-fried Sweet Potato Fries

Ingredients:

- 2 medium sweet potatoes, peeled and cut into fries
- 2 tbsp cornstarch
- Oil for frying
- Salt and pepper, to taste
- Optional: chili powder or paprika for added flavor

Instructions:

1. Heat oil in a deep frying pan or pot over medium heat to 350°F (175°C).
2. Toss the sweet potato fries in cornstarch until evenly coated.
3. Fry the fries in batches until golden brown and crispy, about 4-5 minutes.
4. Remove from oil and drain on paper towels. Season with salt, pepper, and optional chili powder or paprika.
5. Serve hot.

Japanese Pancake (Dorayaki)

Ingredients:

- 1 cup all-purpose flour
- 1 tbsp baking powder
- 1/4 cup sugar
- 2 eggs
- 1/2 cup milk
- 2 tbsp honey
- 1/4 tsp vanilla extract
- Red bean paste (anko) for filling

Instructions:

1. In a bowl, whisk together the flour, baking powder, and sugar.
2. In a separate bowl, beat the eggs, milk, honey, and vanilla extract.
3. Combine the wet and dry ingredients to form a smooth batter.
4. Heat a non-stick pan over medium heat and lightly grease it.
5. Pour small circles of batter onto the pan and cook until bubbles form on the surface (about 1-2 minutes).
6. Flip and cook for another 1-2 minutes until golden brown.
7. Spread a layer of red bean paste on one pancake, then sandwich with another pancake. Serve immediately.

Yaki Tori (Grilled Chicken Skewers)

Ingredients:

- 1 lb chicken thigh, boneless and cut into cubes
- 2 tbsp soy sauce
- 1 tbsp sake
- 1 tbsp mirin
- 1 tbsp honey
- 2 green onions, cut into 2-inch pieces
- Skewers (soaked in water if wooden)

Instructions:

1. In a bowl, mix soy sauce, sake, mirin, and honey to make the marinade.
2. Thread the chicken cubes and green onions onto the skewers alternately.
3. Marinate the skewers for 15-20 minutes.
4. Preheat the grill or grill pan over medium heat.
5. Grill the skewers for 3-4 minutes per side, basting with extra marinade as they cook.
6. Serve with a sprinkle of sesame seeds or green onions.

Sushi Rolls (Street Style)

Ingredients:

- 1 cup sushi rice
- 1 1/4 cups water
- 2 tbsp rice vinegar
- 1 tbsp sugar
- 1 tsp salt
- 4 sheets nori (seaweed)
- Various fillings: cucumber, avocado, crab sticks, tuna, salmon, or pickled radish
- Soy sauce for dipping

Instructions:

1. Rinse the sushi rice until the water runs clear, then cook it according to package instructions.
2. Once cooked, mix rice vinegar, sugar, and salt in a small bowl and stir into the rice. Let cool.
3. Place a sheet of nori on a bamboo mat. Spread a thin layer of rice on top, leaving a small border on one edge.
4. Arrange the fillings along the center of the rice.
5. Roll up the sushi tightly using the bamboo mat. Slice into bite-sized pieces.
6. Serve with soy sauce and pickled ginger.

Ramen Burger

Ingredients:

- 2 ramen noodle blocks (cooked and drained)
- 1 egg (for binding)
- 1/4 cup breadcrumbs
- 1 lb ground beef or pork (for the patty)
- 1 tbsp soy sauce
- Lettuce, tomato, and other toppings
- 2 buns or substitute with cooked ramen for the "bun"

Instructions:

1. In a bowl, mix the cooked ramen with one egg and breadcrumbs. Form into two round "buns."
2. Pan-fry the ramen buns in a lightly greased pan until crispy and golden brown on both sides.
3. In another pan, cook the ground meat into a patty, seasoning with soy sauce.
4. Assemble the ramen burger by placing the patty between the ramen buns, adding lettuce, tomato, and any additional toppings.
5. Serve immediately.

Edamame Beans with Sea Salt

Ingredients:

- 1 lb edamame (young soybeans in pods)
- Sea salt to taste
- Water for boiling

Instructions:

1. Bring a large pot of water to a boil and add the edamame.
2. Boil for 3-5 minutes until the edamame is tender.
3. Drain and sprinkle with sea salt.
4. Serve immediately as a snack or appetizer.

Zaru Soba (Cold Soba Noodles)

Ingredients:

- 8 oz soba noodles
- 2 tbsp soy sauce
- 2 tbsp mirin
- 1/2 cup dashi stock (or water)
- 1 tbsp sugar
- 1 tsp sesame oil
- 1 tbsp chopped scallions
- 1 tbsp toasted sesame seeds (optional)
- Wasabi or pickled ginger (optional)

Instructions:

1. Cook the soba noodles according to package instructions. Drain and rinse them under cold water to stop the cooking process.
2. In a small saucepan, combine soy sauce, mirin, dashi stock, and sugar. Bring to a boil, then reduce to a simmer and cook for 2-3 minutes.
3. Allow the sauce to cool slightly, then add sesame oil and mix well.
4. To serve, arrange the cold soba noodles on a plate or bamboo mat (zaru) and drizzle with the dipping sauce.
5. Garnish with chopped scallions and sesame seeds. Serve with a small dish of wasabi or pickled ginger on the side.

Sweet Potato Pie

Ingredients:

- 1 1/2 lbs sweet potatoes (peeled and cubed)
- 1/2 cup sugar
- 1/4 cup brown sugar
- 1/2 cup milk
- 1/4 cup unsalted butter (melted)
- 2 eggs
- 1 tsp vanilla extract
- 1/2 tsp ground cinnamon
- 1/4 tsp ground nutmeg
- 1/4 tsp salt
- 1 prepared pie crust

Instructions:

1. Preheat the oven to 375°F (190°C).
2. Boil the sweet potatoes in water until soft (about 15-20 minutes). Drain and mash them until smooth.
3. In a bowl, combine mashed sweet potatoes, sugar, brown sugar, milk, melted butter, eggs, vanilla extract, cinnamon, nutmeg, and salt. Mix well until smooth.
4. Pour the sweet potato mixture into the prepared pie crust.

5. Bake for 45-50 minutes, or until the filling is set and slightly golden around the edges.

6. Let the pie cool completely before serving.

Tofu Donburi (Tofu Rice Bowl)

Ingredients:

- 1 block firm tofu, drained and cubed
- 1 tbsp soy sauce
- 1 tbsp sesame oil
- 1 tbsp rice vinegar
- 1/2 tsp sugar
- 2 cups steamed rice (white or brown)
- 1/4 cup sliced scallions
- 1 tbsp toasted sesame seeds
- 1/2 tsp chili flakes (optional)

Instructions:

1. Heat sesame oil in a pan over medium heat. Add cubed tofu and cook until golden on all sides (about 8-10 minutes).
2. In a small bowl, whisk together soy sauce, rice vinegar, sugar, and chili flakes (if using).
3. Once the tofu is browned, pour the soy sauce mixture over the tofu and cook for another 2-3 minutes until the sauce thickens.
4. Serve the tofu mixture over a bowl of steamed rice, garnished with scallions and toasted sesame seeds.

Hokkaido Cream Puffs

Ingredients for the Choux Pastry:

- 1/2 cup water
- 1/2 cup milk
- 1/2 cup unsalted butter
- 1 tsp vanilla extract
- 1 cup all-purpose flour
- 4 large eggs

Ingredients for the Cream Filling:

- 1 cup heavy cream
- 1/4 cup powdered sugar
- 1 tsp vanilla extract

Instructions:

1. Preheat the oven to 400°F (200°C) and line a baking sheet with parchment paper.
2. In a saucepan, combine water, milk, butter, and vanilla extract. Bring to a boil, then remove from heat.
3. Stir in the flour all at once and return the pan to medium heat. Stir constantly until the dough forms a smooth ball and pulls away from the sides of the pan.
4. Remove from heat and let it cool slightly. Add the eggs one at a time, mixing well after each addition until the dough is smooth and glossy.

5. Using a spoon or piping bag, form small mounds of dough on the baking sheet. Bake for 20-25 minutes or until golden and puffed. Allow to cool.

6. To make the filling, whip the heavy cream with powdered sugar and vanilla extract until soft peaks form.

7. Once the cream puffs have cooled, carefully slice them in half and fill them with the whipped cream.

8. Dust with powdered sugar before serving.

Mentaiko (Spicy Cod Roe) on Rice

Ingredients:

- 1/4 cup mentaiko (spicy cod roe)
- 1 bowl steamed rice (white or brown)
- 1 tbsp soy sauce
- 1 tsp sesame oil
- 1/2 tsp chili oil (optional)
- Chopped nori (seaweed) for garnish
- Scallions for garnish

Instructions:

1. Cook the rice and transfer it to a bowl.
2. Mix mentaiko with soy sauce, sesame oil, and chili oil (if using).
3. Spoon the mentaiko mixture over the hot rice.
4. Garnish with chopped nori and scallions.
5. Serve immediately, enjoying the bold flavors.

Japanese French Fries

Ingredients:

- 2 large potatoes (peeled and cut into fries)
- 1 tbsp cornstarch
- Oil for frying
- Salt to taste
- Optional: chili powder or wasabi powder

Instructions:

1. Heat oil in a deep fryer or large pot to 350°F (175°C).
2. Toss the cut fries in cornstarch to coat evenly.
3. Fry the fries in batches for about 4-5 minutes or until golden brown and crispy.
4. Remove from oil and drain on paper towels. Season with salt and optional chili powder or wasabi powder for a kick.
5. Serve hot as a snack or side dish.

Yuba (Tofu Skin) Snack

Ingredients:

- 1 pack yuba (tofu skin)
- 1 tbsp soy sauce
- 1 tsp sesame oil
- 1 tsp rice vinegar
- 1 tsp honey
- 1 tsp toasted sesame seeds (optional)

Instructions:

1. In a small bowl, mix soy sauce, sesame oil, rice vinegar, and honey to create a dipping sauce.
2. Gently heat the yuba in a pan with a little bit of sesame oil until warm.
3. Cut the yuba into strips or bite-sized pieces.
4. Drizzle with the dipping sauce and sprinkle with toasted sesame seeds.
5. Serve immediately as a light snack or appetizer.

Shoyu Ice Cream (Soy Sauce Ice Cream)

Ingredients:

- 2 cups heavy cream
- 1 cup whole milk
- 3/4 cup sugar
- 1 tbsp soy sauce (shoyu)
- 1 tsp vanilla extract

Instructions:

1. In a bowl, whisk together the milk and sugar until dissolved.
2. Stir in heavy cream, soy sauce, and vanilla.
3. Chill the mixture in the fridge for at least 2 hours.
4. Pour into an ice cream maker and churn according to the manufacturer's instructions.
5. Freeze for an additional 2-4 hours before serving. The soy sauce gives a subtle umami-caramel flavor.

Sweet Red Bean Paste-filled Buns (Anpan)

Ingredients:

- 2 cups all-purpose flour
- 2 tbsp sugar
- 1 tsp yeast
- 1/2 tsp salt
- 3/4 cup warm milk
- 2 tbsp butter, softened
- 1 cup anko (sweet red bean paste)

Instructions:

1. Mix flour, sugar, salt, and yeast. Gradually add warm milk and mix into a dough.
2. Knead for 8–10 minutes, then incorporate the butter. Let rise for 1 hour.
3. Divide into equal balls, flatten each, and place a tablespoon of anko in the center.
4. Seal and place seam-side down. Let rise again for 30 minutes.
5. Bake at 350°F (175°C) for 15–18 minutes until golden. Cool slightly before eating.

Yaki Udon (Fried Udon Noodles)

Ingredients:

- 1 pack udon noodles
- 1/2 onion, sliced
- 1/2 cup cabbage, shredded
- 1/2 cup sliced mushrooms
- 2 tbsp soy sauce
- 1 tbsp oyster sauce
- 1 tbsp sesame oil
- Optional: pork, beef, or tofu
- Green onions and sesame seeds for garnish

Instructions:

1. Heat sesame oil in a pan, sauté onions and mushrooms until soft.
2. Add cabbage and protein of choice. Stir-fry until cooked.
3. Add udon noodles and toss in soy sauce and oyster sauce. Stir-fry for 3–5 minutes.
4. Serve hot, topped with scallions and sesame seeds.

Matcha-flavored Mochi

Ingredients:

- 1 cup glutinous rice flour
- 1/4 cup sugar
- 1 tsp matcha powder
- 3/4 cup water
- Potato starch for dusting

Instructions:

1. Mix glutinous rice flour, sugar, and matcha powder. Gradually stir in water until smooth.
2. Microwave for 2 minutes, stir, then microwave another 1–2 minutes until sticky.
3. Dust a surface with potato starch and transfer the mochi.
4. Divide and shape into small balls. Can be filled with red bean paste or enjoyed plain.

Japanese Street Pizza (Okonomiyaki-style)

Ingredients:

- 1 cup flour
- 1 egg
- 1/2 cup dashi or water
- 1 cup shredded cabbage
- 1/4 cup chopped green onion
- Optional: bacon, shrimp, or cheese
- Toppings: okonomiyaki sauce, mayo, bonito flakes, aonori

Instructions:

1. Mix flour, egg, and dashi into a batter.
2. Add cabbage, green onion, and any optional fillings.
3. Pour batter into a hot, greased skillet and cook both sides until golden brown.
4. Drizzle with okonomiyaki sauce, mayo, and sprinkle with bonito flakes and aonori.

Baked Custard Pudding (Purin)

Ingredients:

- 2 cups milk
- 3 eggs
- 1/3 cup sugar
- 1 tsp vanilla extract
- For caramel: 1/3 cup sugar + 2 tbsp water

Instructions:

1. Make caramel by heating sugar and water until golden brown. Pour into ramekins.
2. In a saucepan, heat milk until warm. Whisk eggs and sugar, then slowly add the warm milk and vanilla.
3. Strain the mixture and pour into the ramekins.
4. Bake in a water bath at 325°F (160°C) for 30–40 minutes.
5. Chill before serving, invert to release the custard with caramel on top.

Dorayaki (Red Bean Pancake Sandwich)

Ingredients:

- 2 eggs
- 1/2 cup sugar
- 1 tbsp honey
- 3/4 cup all-purpose flour
- 1/2 tsp baking powder
- 1–2 tbsp water
- 1 cup anko (sweet red bean paste)

Instructions:

1. Whisk eggs, sugar, and honey until fluffy. Add sifted flour and baking powder.
2. Mix and add water as needed to form pancake batter.
3. Cook small pancakes on a lightly oiled pan over medium-low heat.
4. Sandwich two pancakes with a spoonful of anko in the middle.

Jaga Bata (Potatoes with Butter and Soy Sauce)

Ingredients:

- 2 large potatoes
- 2 tbsp butter
- 1 tbsp soy sauce
- Optional: corn kernels, chopped parsley, or bonito flakes

Instructions:

1. Boil or steam whole potatoes until tender. Peel if desired.
2. Cut into halves or quarters and place in a skillet with butter.
3. Drizzle soy sauce over the hot potatoes and let it slightly caramelize.
4. Garnish with corn, parsley, or bonito flakes and serve immediately.

Anko-filled Taiyaki (Fish-shaped Pancake with Red Bean)

Ingredients:

- 1 cup all-purpose flour
- 1 egg
- 3/4 cup milk
- 2 tbsp sugar
- 1/2 tsp baking powder
- 1 cup anko (sweet red bean paste)
- Taiyaki mold

Instructions:

1. Mix flour, sugar, baking powder, egg, and milk to create a pancake batter.
2. Heat the taiyaki mold and lightly grease it.
3. Pour a thin layer of batter, add 1 tbsp anko in the center, and cover with more batter.
4. Close the mold and cook 2–3 minutes per side, until golden brown.

Asparagus Wrapped in Bacon

Ingredients:

- 1 bunch of asparagus, trimmed
- 8–10 slices of thin bacon
- Black pepper, to taste

Instructions:

1. Wrap each asparagus stalk with a strip of bacon.
2. Grill, pan-fry, or bake at 400°F (200°C) for 15 minutes, turning halfway.
3. Sprinkle with black pepper and serve hot as a side or appetizer.

Tempura Fish Balls

Ingredients:

- 1 lb white fish fillet (cod, pollock), minced
- 1 egg white
- 1 tbsp sake
- 1/2 tsp salt
- 2 tbsp cornstarch
- For batter: 1/2 cup flour, 1/2 cup cold water, 1 egg yolk

Instructions:

1. Mix fish, egg white, sake, salt, and cornstarch. Shape into small balls.
2. Whisk together batter ingredients until just combined (don't overmix).
3. Dip balls into batter and deep-fry at 350°F (175°C) until golden and crisp.
4. Serve with tentsuyu dipping sauce or a soy-chili dip.

Japanese Cheese Tarts

Ingredients:

- Tart shells (pre-baked)
- 1/2 cup cream cheese
- 1/4 cup mascarpone
- 2 tbsp sugar
- 1 egg yolk
- 1 tbsp lemon juice
- 1 tbsp heavy cream

Instructions:

1. Beat cream cheese, mascarpone, and sugar until smooth.
2. Add egg yolk, lemon juice, and cream. Mix until well combined.
3. Pour into tart shells and bake at 375°F (190°C) for 10–12 minutes.
4. Let cool before serving. Best enjoyed slightly chilled!

Rice Paper Spring Rolls (Japanese-style with Soy-Sesame Dip)

Ingredients:

- Rice paper sheets
- Cooked shrimp or tofu
- Vermicelli noodles
- Lettuce, cucumber, carrot, and avocado
- Optional: shiso leaves or perilla

Dipping Sauce:

- 2 tbsp soy sauce
- 1 tbsp rice vinegar
- 1 tsp sesame oil
- 1 tsp sugar
- Chili flakes or minced garlic (optional)

Instructions:

1. Soak rice paper in warm water until pliable.
2. Place fillings in the center and roll tightly, folding in the sides.
3. Mix sauce ingredients and serve with the rolls.

www.ingramcontent.com/pod-product-compliance
Lightning Source LLC
LaVergne TN
LVHW061950070526
838199LV00060B/4050